easy meals

one pot

BARNES
&NOBLE
BOOKS
NEW YORK

This edition published by Barnes & Noble Inc.,
by arrangement with Parragon

2002 Barnes & Noble Books

M 1 0 9 8 7 6 5 4 3 2 1

ISBN: 0-7607-3295-7

Printed in Spain

Produced by The Bridgewater Book Company Ltd, Lewes, East Sussex, United Kingdom

Acknowledgements
Creative Director Terry Jeavons
Art Director Sarah Howerd
Editorial Director Fiona Biggs
Senior Editor Mark Truman
Editorial Assistants Simon Bailey, Tom Kitch
Page Make-up Chris Akroyd

NOTES FOR THE READER

- This book uses both metric and US measurements. Follow the same units of measurement throughout; do not mix metric and US measurements.
- All spoon measurements are level: teaspoons are assumed to be 5 ml, and tablespoons are assumed to be 15 ml.
- Cup measurements in this book are for American cups.
- Unless otherwise stated, milk is assumed to be whole milk, eggs and individual vegetables such as potatoes are medium-sized, and pepper is freshly ground black pepper.
- Recipes using raw or very lightly cooked eggs should be avoided by infants, the elderly, pregnant women, convalescents, and anyone suffering from an illness.
- Optional ingredients, variations, and serving suggestions have not been included in the calculations.
- The times given are an approximate guide only. Preparation times differ according to the techniques used by different people and the cooking times vary as a result of the type of oven used.

Contents

Introduction

A collection of delicious recipes which are really easy to prepare and cook is a boon for anyone who has little time to spend in the kitchen or who needs an idea for a filling dish that can be prepared in minutes. All the dishes in this book are substantial enough to make a meal. They range from thick soups, such as Spicy Lamb Soup with Chickpeas & Zucchini, bursting with hearty ingredients, to Golden Chicken Risotto and Azerbaijani Lamb Pilaf, which make wonderful main meals. The collection includes some new and exciting recipes based on vegetables, such as Cashew Nut Paella and Spiced Lentils with Spinach. All the dishes can be cooked in one pot, so there is no juggling with half-a-dozen pans, and no huge pile of pans to wash afterward.

Choose the right recipe, and half an hour after returning home from work you could be sitting down to a delicious Seafood Stew

guide to recipe key	
very easy	Recipes are graded as follows: 1 pea—easy; 2 peas—very easy; 3 peas—extremely easy.
serves 4	Most of the recipes in this book serve four people. Simply halve the ingredients to serve two, taking care not to mix US and metric measurements.
15 minutes	Preparation time. Where marinating or soaking are involved, these times have been added on separately: e.g., 15 minutes, plus 30 minutes to marinate.
15 minutes	Cooking time.

or Chinese Fried Rice. Alternatively, you could throw the ingredients for a Lamb Hot Pot or a Chickpea & Vegetable Casserole into a pot, then relax in the bath, or catch up with friends while it cooks. Baked Tomato Rice with Sausages takes only 15 minutes to prepare, and the dish is tasty and filling.

One-pot meals eliminate hours of preparation when cooking for guests. A menu of Chinese Pork Balls & Greens in Broth, followed by Spicy Coconut Rice with Monkfish & Peas, and Osso Bucco with Citrus Zests, makes stylish dinner party fare for friends.

Stir-Fried Squid with Hot Black Bean Sauce, page 62

Soups & Appetizers

The recipes in this section need a minimum of preparation. The ingredients of these soups do not need to be separately cooked, then mixed together in a blender or a food processor, before reheating. Instead, meat, vegetables, beans, and grains are all cooked together. Served with hunks of bread, each soup makes a complete meal. Beef Goulash Soup makes a filling lunch or evening meal. Vegetable Chili, and Vegetable Soup with Bulgur Wheat & Herbs were both created with vegetarians in mind.

Beef Goulash Soup

INGREDIENTS

1 tbsp oil
1 lb 2 oz/500 g lean
  ground beef
2 onions, chopped finely
2 garlic cloves, chopped
  finely
2 tbsp all-purpose flour
1 cup water
14 oz/400 g canned
  chopped tomatoes
  in juice
1 carrot, chopped finely
8 oz/225 g red bell
  pepper, roasted,
  peeled, seeded, and
  chopped
1 tsp Hungarian paprika
¼ tsp caraway seeds
pinch of dried oregano
4 cups beef bouillon
60 g/2¼ oz tagliatelle,
  broken into small
  pieces
salt and pepper
sour cream and fresh
  cilantro, to garnish

❶ Heat the oil in a large wide pan over a medium–high heat. Add the beef and sprinkle with salt and pepper. Panfry until lightly browned.

❷ Reduce the heat and add the onions and garlic. Panfry for about 3 minutes, stirring frequently, until the onions are softened. Stir in the flour and continue cooking the beef and onions for 1 minute.

❸ Add the water and stir to combine, scraping the bottom of the pan to mix in the flour. Stir in the tomatoes, carrot, bell pepper, paprika, caraway seeds, oregano, and bouillon.

❹ Bring just to a boil. Reduce the heat, cover the pan and simmer gently for about 40 minutes, stirring occasionally, until all the vegetables are tender.

❺ Add the tagliatelle to the soup and simmer for another 20 minutes, or until the pasta is cooked.

❻ Taste the soup and adjust the seasoning, if necessary. Ladle into warm bowls and top each with a tablespoon of sour cream. Garnish with cilantro.

 extremely easy

 serves 4

 10 minutes

 1 hour,
20 minutes

8

Chinese Pork Balls & Greens in Broth

INGREDIENTS

8 cups chicken bouillon
3 oz/85 g shiitake
   mushrooms, sliced
   thinly
6 oz/175 g bok choy or
   other Chinese greens,
   sliced into thin
   ribbons
6 scallions, sliced finely
salt and pepper

PORK BALLS
8 oz/225 g lean ground
   pork
1 oz/25 g fresh spinach
   leaves, chopped finely
2 scallions, chopped
   finely
1 garlic clove, chopped
   very finely
pinch of Chinese 5-spice
   powder
1 tsp soy sauce

❶ To make the pork balls, put the pork, spinach, scallions, and garlic in a bowl. Add the 5-spice powder and soy and mix until well combined.

❷ Shape the pork mixture into 24 balls. Place them in one layer in a steamer that will fit over the top of a pan.

❸ Bring the bouillon just to a boil in a pan that will accommodate the steamer. Regulate the heat so that the liquid bubbles gently. Add the mushrooms to the bouillon and place the steamer, covered, on top of the pan. Steam for 10 minutes. Remove the steamer and set aside on a plate.

❹ Add the bok choy or greens and scallions to the pan, and cook gently in the bouillon for 3–4 minutes, or until the leaves are wilted. Taste the soup and adjust the seasoning, if necessary, to taste.

❺ Divide the pork balls evenly among 6 warm bowls and ladle the soup over them. Serve at once.

 very easy

 serves 6

15 minutes

25–30 minutes

Spicy Lamb Soup with Chickpeas & Zucchini

1–2 tbsp olive oil

1 lb/450 g lean boneless lamb, such as shoulder or neck fillet, trimmed of fat and cut into ½ inch/1 cm cubes

1 onion, chopped finely

2–3 garlic cloves, crushed

5 cups water

14 oz/400 g canned chopped tomatoes in juice

1 bay leaf

½ tsp dried thyme

½ tsp dried oregano

⅛ tsp ground cinnamon

¼ tsp ground cumin

¼ tsp ground turmeric

1 tsp harissa, or more to taste

14 oz/400 g canned chickpeas, drained and rinsed

1 carrot, diced

1 potato, diced

1 zucchini, cut into fourths and sliced lengthwise

3½ oz/100 g fresh green peas, or frozen peas, defrosted

chopped fresh mint or cilantro, to garnish

easy

serves 4

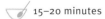

15–20 minutes

about 2 hours

❶ Heat the oil in a large pan or a cast-iron casserole over a medium–high heat. Add the lamb, in batches if necessary to avoid crowding the pan, and cook until evenly browned on all sides, adding a little more oil if needed. Remove the meat with a slotted spoon when browned.

❷ Reduce the heat and add the onion and garlic to the pan. Cook, stirring frequently, for 1–2 minutes.

❸ Add the water and return all the meat to the pan. Bring just to a boil and skim off any foam that rises to the surface. Reduce the heat and stir in the tomatoes, bay leaf, thyme, oregano, cinnamon, cumin, turmeric, and harissa. Simmer for about 1 hour, or until the meat is very tender. Discard the bay leaf.

❹ Stir in the chickpeas, carrot, and potato, and simmer for 15 minutes. Add the zucchini and peas, and continue simmering for 15–20 minutes, or until all the vegetables are tender.

❺ Adjust the seasoning, adding more harissa, if desired. Ladle the soup into warm bowls and garnish with chopped mint or cilantro leaves.

Turkey Soup with Rice, Mushrooms & Sage

INGREDIENTS

3 tbsp butter
1 onion, chopped finely
1 celery stalk, chopped
    finely
25 large fresh sage
    leaves, chopped finely
4 tbsp all-purpose flour
5 cups turkey or chicken
    bouillon
3½ oz/100 g rice
9 oz/250 g mushrooms,
    sliced
7 oz/200 g cooked turkey
¾ cup heavy cream
freshly grated Parmesan
    cheese, to serve

❶ Melt half the butter in a large pan over a medium–low heat. Add the onion, celery, and sage, and panfry for 3–4 minutes, or until the onion is softened, stirring frequently. Stir in the flour and continue cooking for 2 minutes.

❷ Add about one fourth of the bouillon, a little at a time, and stir well, scraping the bottom of the pan to mix in the flour. Pour in the remaining bouillon, stirring to combine completely, and bring just to a boil.

❸ Stir in the rice, and season to taste. Reduce the heat and simmer gently, partially covered, for about 30 minutes, or until the rice is just tender, stirring occasionally.

❹ Meanwhile, melt the remaining butter in a large skillet over a medium heat. Add the mushrooms, and season with salt and pepper. Cook for about 8 minutes, or until they are golden brown, stirring occasionally at first, then more often after they start to color. Add the mushrooms to the soup.

❺ Add the turkey to the soup and stir in the cream. Continue simmering for about 10 minutes, or until heated through. Taste and adjust the seasoning, if necessary. Ladle into the soup into warm bowls and serve with freshly grated Parmesan cheese.

very easy

serves 4

10 minutes

about 1 hour

Minestrone

INGREDIENTS

1 tbsp olive oil
1 onion, chopped finely
1 leek, sliced thinly
2 garlic cloves, chopped
   finely
14 oz/400 g canned
   chopped tomatoes
1 carrot, diced finely
1 small turnip, diced finely
1 small potato, diced
   finely
4½ oz/125 g peeled celery
   root, diced finely
9 oz/250 g peeled
   pumpkin flesh, diced
   finely
3 cups water
4 cups chicken or
   vegetable bouillon
14 oz/400 g canned
   cannellini or borlotti
   beans, drained and
   rinsed
3½ oz/100 g leafy
   cabbage, such as
   cavolo nero
3 oz/85 g small pasta
   shapes or broken
   spaghetti
salt and pepper
freshly grated Parmesan
   cheese, to serve

❶ Heat the oil in a large pan over a medium heat. Add the onion, leek, and garlic, and panfry for 3–4 minutes, stirring occasionally, until slightly softened.

❷ Add the tomatoes, carrot, turnip, potato, celery root, pumpkin, water, and bouillon. Bring to a boil, stirring occasionally.

❸ Stir the beans and cabbage into the pan. Season lightly with salt and pepper. Reduce the heat and simmer, partially covered, for about 50 minutes, or until all the vegetables are tender.

❹ Bring salted water to a boil in a pan. Add the pasta and cook until just tender. Drain the pasta and add it to the soup.

❺ Taste the soup and adjust the seasoning. Ladle into warm bowls and serve with freshly grated Parmesan cheese.

 extremely easy

 serves 4

 20 minutes

 1 hour,
10 minutes

Vegetable Chili

INGREDIENTS

1 medium eggplant,
  peeled if wished, cut
  into 1 inch/2.5 cm
  slices
1 tbsp olive oil, plus extra
  for brushing
1 large red or yellow
  onion, chopped finely
2 bell peppers, chopped
  finely
3–4 garlic cloves,
  chopped finely or
  crushed
800 g/28 oz canned
  chopped tomatoes
  in juice
1 tbsp mild chili powder,
  or to taste
½ tsp ground cumin
½ tsp dried oregano
2 small zucchini, cut into
  fourths lengthwise
  and sliced
14 oz/400 g canned
  kidney beans, drained
  and rinsed
2 cups water
1 tbsp tomato paste
6 scallions, chopped
  finely
4 oz/115 g grated
  Cheddar cheese
salt and pepper

easy

serves 4

15 minutes

1 hour,
25 minutes

❶ Brush the eggplant slices on one side with olive oil. Heat half the oil in a large skillet over a medium–high heat. Add the eggplant, oiled side up, and cook for 5–6 minutes, or until browned on one side. Turn, brown the other side, transfer to a plate, and cut into bite-sized pieces.

❷ Heat the remaining oil in a large pan over a medium heat. Add the onion and bell peppers, cover, and cook for 3–4 minutes, stirring occasionally, until the onion is just softened. Add the garlic and continue cooking for 2–3 minutes, or until the onion begins to color.

❸ Add the tomatoes, chili powder, cumin, and oregano. Season with salt and pepper. Bring just to a boil and reduce the heat, then cover and simmer for 15 minutes.

❹ Add the zucchini, eggplant pieces, and beans. Stir in the water and the tomato paste. Cover again and continue simmering for about 45 minutes, or until the vegetables are tender. Taste and adjust the seasoning. If you prefer a spicier chili, stir in a little more chili powder.

❺ Season to taste. Ladle the chili into bowls and top with scallions and cheese.

Mushroom & Barley Soup

INGREDIENTS

60 g/2¼ oz pearl barley
6¼ cups chicken or
    vegetable bouillon
1 bay leaf
1 tbsp butter
12 oz/350 g mushrooms,
    sliced thinly
1 tsp olive oil
1 onion, chopped finely
2 carrots, sliced thinly
1 tbsp chopped fresh
    tarragon
1 tbsp chopped fresh
    parsley or tarragon,
    to garnish

❶ Rinse the barley and drain. Bring 2 cups of the bouillon to a boil in a small pan. Add the bay leaf and, if the bouillon is unsalted, add a large pinch of salt. Stir in the barley, then reduce the heat, cover, and simmer for 40 minutes.

❷ Melt the butter in a large skillet over a medium heat. Add the mushrooms and season with salt and pepper. Cook for about 8 minutes, or until they are golden brown, stirring occasionally at first, then more often after they start to color. Remove the mushrooms from the heat.

❸ Heat the oil in a large pan over a medium heat and add the onion and carrots. Cover and cook for about 3 minutes, stirring frequently, until the onion is softened.

❹ Add the remaining bouillon and bring to a boil. Stir in the barley with its cooking liquid, and add the mushrooms. Reduce the heat, cover the pan, and simmer gently for about 20 minutes, or until the carrots are tender, stirring the pan occasionally.

❺ Stir in the chopped tarragon. Taste and adjust the seasoning, if necessary. Ladle into warm bowls, then garnish with fresh parsley or tarragon, and serve.

 very easy

 serves 4

 10 minutes

 1¼ hours

Vegetable Soup with Bulgur Wheat & Herbs

INGREDIENTS

1 tbsp olive oil
2 onions, chopped
3 garlic cloves, chopped
   finely or crushed
⅓ cup bulgur wheat
5 tomatoes, skinned and
   sliced, or 14 oz/400 g
   canned plum
   tomatoes in juice
8 oz/225 g peeled
   pumpkin or acorn
   squash, diced
1 large zucchini, cut into
   fourths lengthwise
   and sliced
4 cups boiling water
2 tbsp tomato paste
¼ tsp chili paste
1½ oz/40 g chopped
   mixed fresh oregano,
   basil, and flatleaf
   parsley
1 oz/25 g arugula leaves,
   chopped roughly
1⅓ cups shelled fresh or
   frozen peas
salt and pepper
freshly grated Parmesan
   cheese, to serve

❶ Heat the oil in a large pan over a medium–low heat and add the onions and garlic. Cover and cook for 5–8 minutes, or until the onions soften.

❷ Stir in the bulgur wheat and continue cooking for 1 minute.

❸ Layer the tomatoes, pumpkin or squash, and zucchini in the pan.

❹ Combine half the water with the tomato paste, chili paste, and a large pinch of salt. Pour the liquid over the vegetables. Cover the pan and simmer for 15 minutes.

❺ Uncover the pan and stir. Put all the herbs and the arugula on top of the soup and layer the peas over them. Pour over the remaining water and gently bring to a boil. Reduce the heat and simmer for about 20–25 minutes, or until all the vegetables are tender.

❻ Stir the soup. Taste and adjust the seasoning, adding salt and pepper if necessary, and a little more chili paste if you wish. Ladle into warm bowls and serve with Parmesan cheese.

easy

serves 4

10 minutes

1 hour

Main
Meals

These dishes are cooked in just one pot, so that all the goodness and flavor of the ingredients are cooked into the soup. Simmered Stew of Meat, Chicken, Vegetables & Fruit is a dish that contains proteins and vitamins, and its fruit gives it an intriguing taste and texture. The classic stews such as Lamb Hot Pot and the wonderful Maltese Rabbit with Fennel can be left unattended to simmer slowly. By contrast, Stir-fried Squid with Hot Black Bean Sauce takes only minutes to toss in a wok. This Eastern cooking method is not only fast but also healthy and versatile.

Osso Bucco with Citrus Zest

INGREDIENTS

1–2 tbsp all-purpose
  flour
6 meaty slices osso
  bucco (veal shins)
2 lb 4 oz/1 kg fresh
  tomatoes, skinned,
  seeded, and diced, or
  28 oz/800 g canned
  chopped tomatoes
1–2 tbsp olive oil
9 oz/250 g onions,
  chopped very finely
9 oz/250 g carrots, diced
  finely
1 cup dry white wine
1 cup veal bouillon
6 large basil leaves
1 large garlic clove,
  chopped very finely
finely grated zest of
  1 large lemon
finely grated zest of
  1 orange
2 tbsp finely chopped
  fresh flatleaf parsley
salt and pepper

❶ Put the flour in a plastic bag and season with salt and pepper. Add the osso bucco, a couple of pieces at a time, and shake until well coated. Remove and shake off the excess flour. Continue until all the pieces are coated.

❷ If using canned tomatoes, empty the can into a strainer and let drain.

❸ Heat 1 tablespoon of the oil in a large flameproof casserole. Add the osso bucco and cook for 10 minutes on each side until well browned. Remove from the casserole.

❹ Add 1–2 teaspoons of oil to the casserole if necessary. Add the onions and cook for about 5 minutes, stirring, until soft. Stir in the carrots and panfry until they soften.

❺ Add the tomatoes, wine, bouillon, and basil, and return the osso bucco to the pan. Bring to a boil, then lower the heat and simmer for 1 hour, covered. Check that the meat is tender with the tip of a knife. If not, continue cooking for 10 minutes and test again. When the meat is tender, sprinkle with the garlic and lemon and orange zest, then cover the pan again and cook for another 10 minutes.

❻ Adjust the seasoning if necessary. Sprinkle with the parsley, and serve.

 easy

 serves 4

20 minutes

1¾ hours

Spanish Chicken with Garlic

INGREDIENTS

2–3 tbsp all-purpose flour
cayenne pepper
4 chicken chicken joints, patted dry
about 4 tbsp olive oil
20 large garlic cloves, each halved and the green core removed
1 large bay leaf
2 cups chicken bouillon
4 tbsp dry white wine
chopped fresh parsley, to garnish
salt and pepper

❶ Put about 2 tablespoons of the flour in a bag and season to taste with cayenne pepper and salt and pepper. Add a chicken piece and shake until it is lightly coated with the flour, shaking off the excess. Repeat with the remaining pieces, adding more flour and seasoning, if necessary.

❷ Heat 3 tablespoons of the olive oil in a large skillet. Add the garlic cloves and cook for about 2 minutes, stirring, to flavor the oil. Remove with a slotted spoon and set aside.

❸ Add the chicken to the pan, skin-side down, and panfry for 5 minutes, or until golden brown. Turn and cook for an additional 5 minutes, adding 1–2 tablespoons of oil if needed.

❹ Return the garlic to the pan. Add the bay leaf, chicken bouillon, and wine, and bring to a boil. Lower the heat, cover the pan and simmer for 25 minutes, or until the chicken is tender and the garlic cloves are very soft. Using a slotted spoon, transfer the chicken to a serving plate and keep warm. Bring the cooking liquid to a boil with the garlic, and boil until reduced to about 1 cup plus 2 tablespoons. Adjust the seasoning, if necessary.

❺ Spoon the sauce over the chicken pieces and scatter the garlic cloves around. Garnish with parsley and serve.

very easy

serves 4

10 minutes

1 hour

Basque Pork & Beans

INGREDIENTS

7 oz/200 g dried
   cannellini beans,
   soaked overnight
olive oil
600 g/1 lb 5 oz boneless
   leg of pork, cut into
   2 inch/5 cm chunks
1 large onion, sliced
3 large garlic cloves,
   crushed
14 oz/400 g canned
   chopped tomatoes
2 green bell peppers,
   cored, seeded, and
   sliced
finely grated zest of
   1 large orange
salt and pepper
finely chopped fresh
   parsley, to garnish

❶ Drain the cannellini beans and put in a large pan with fresh water to cover. Bring to a boil and boil rapidly for 10 minutes. Lower the heat and simmer for 20 minutes. Drain and set aside.

❷ Add enough oil to cover the base of a skillet in a very thin layer. Heat the oil over medium heat, add a few pieces of the pork, and panfry on all sides, until brown. Repeat with the remaining pork and set aside.

❸ Add 1 tablespoon of oil to the skillet, if needed, then add the onion and cook for 3 minutes. Stir in the garlic and cook for an additional 2 minutes. Return the pork to the skillet.

❹ Add the tomatoes to the skillet and bring to a boil. Lower the heat, then stir in the bell pepper slices, orange zest, drained beans, and salt and pepper to taste.

❺ Transfer the contents of the skillet to a casserole.

❻ Cover the casserole and cook in a preheated oven at 350°F/180°C for 45 minutes, or until the beans and pork are tender. Sprinkle with parsley and serve.

 very easy

 serves 4

 15 minutes

 1 hour,
20 minutes

Maltese Rabbit with Fennel

5 tbsp olive oil
2 large fennel bulbs,
    trimmed and sliced
2 carrots, diced
1 large garlic clove,
    crushed
1 tbsp fennel seeds
about 4 tbsp all-purpose
    flour
2 wild rabbits, jointed
1 cup dry white wine
1 cup water
1 bouquet garni of
    2 sprigs fresh flatleaf
    parsley, 1 sprig fresh
    rosemary, and 1 bay
    leaf, tied in a 3 inch/
    7.5 cm piece of celery
salt and pepper
thick, crusty bread,
    to serve

TO GARNISH
finely chopped fresh
    flatleaf parsley or
    cilantro
fresh rosemary sprigs

❶ Heat 3 tablespoons of the olive oil in a large flameproof casserole. Add the fennel and carrots, and cook them for 5 minutes, stirring occasionally. Stir in the garlic and fennel seeds, and cook for 2 minutes, or until the fennel is tender. Remove the fennel and carrots, and set aside.

❷ Put 4 tablespoons of flour in a plastic bag, and add seasoning. Add 2 rabbit pieces and shake to coat lightly, then shake off any excess flour. Continue until all the pieces of rabbit are coated, adding more flour, if necessary.

❸ Add the remaining oil to the casserole. Cook the rabbit pieces for about 5 minutes on each side, or until golden brown, working in batches. Remove the rabbit from the casserole as it cooks.

❹ Pour in the wine, and bubble the mixture over the heat, stirring the bottom of the casserole hard. Return the rabbit pieces, fennel, and carrots to the casserole, and pour in the water. Add the bouquet garni and salt and pepper to taste.

❺ Bring to a boil. Lower the heat, cover the pan, and simmer for about 1¼ hours, or until the rabbit is tender.

❻ Discard the bouquet garni. Garnish with herbs and serve straight from the casserole with plenty of bread.

easy

serves 4

15 minutes

1¾ hours

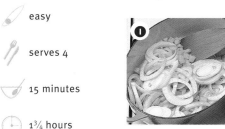

Chicken Basquaise

3 lb/1.3 kg chicken, cut into 8 pieces
flour, for dusting
3 tbsp olive oil
1 large onion, (preferably Spanish), sliced thickly
2 bell peppers, seeded and cut lengthwise into thick strips
2 garlic cloves
5½ oz/150 g spicy chorizo sausage, peeled, if necessary, and cut into ½ inch/1 cm pieces
1 tbsp tomato paste
1 cup long-grain white rice or medium-grain Spanish rice, such as valencia
2 cups chicken bouillon
1 tsp crushed dried chilis
½ tsp dried thyme
4 oz/115 g Bayonne or other air-dried ham, diced
12 dry-cured black olives
2 tbsp chopped fresh flatleaf parsley
salt and pepper

very easy

serves 4

10 minutes

1½ hours

❶ Dry the chicken pieces well with paper towels. Put about 2 tablespoons of flour in a plastic bag and season with salt and pepper, then add the chicken pieces. Seal the bag and shake to coat the chicken.

❷ Heat 2 tablespoons of the oil in a flameproof casserole over a medium–high heat. Add the chicken and cook for about 15 minutes, or until well browned. Transfer to a plate.

❸ Heat the remaining oil in the pan and add the onion and bell peppers. Reduce the heat to medium and stir-fry until they begin to color and soften. Add the garlic, chorizo, and tomato paste, and continue stirring for about 3 minutes. Add the rice and cook for about 2 minutes, stirring to coat, until the rice is translucent.

❹ Add the bouillon, crushed chilis, thyme, and salt and pepper, and stir. Bring to a boil. Return the chicken to the pan, pressing gently into the rice. Cover, and cook over a very low heat for about 45 minutes, or until the chicken and rice are tender.

❺ Stir the ham, black olives, and half the parsley gently into the rice mixture. Cover the pan and heat through for another 5 minutes. Sprinkle the chicken and vegetables with the remaining parsley, and serve.

Azerbaijani Lamb Pilaf

INGREDIENTS

2–3 tbsp oil
1 lb 7 oz/650 g boneless
    lamb shoulder, cut
    into 1 inch/2.5 cm
    cubes
2 onions, chopped
    roughly
1 tsp ground cumin
7 oz/200 g risotto, long-
    grain, or basmati rice
1 tbsp tomato paste
1 tsp saffron threads
scant ½ cup
    pomegranate juice
3¾ cups lamb or chicken
    bouillon, or water
4 oz/115 g dried apricots
    or prunes, ready
    soaked and halved
2 tbsp raisins
salt and pepper

TO SERVE
2 tbsp chopped fresh
    mint
2 tbsp chopped fresh
    watercress

❶ Heat the oil in a large flameproof casserole or a wide pan over a high heat. Add the lamb in batches and cook for about 7 minutes, turning, until lightly browned.

❷ Add the onions to the casserole, then reduce the heat to medium–high and cook for about 2 minutes, or until they begin to soften. Add the cumin and rice and cook for about 2 minutes, stirring to coat well, until the rice is translucent. Stir in the tomato paste and the saffron threads.

❸ Add the pomegranate juice and bouillon, and bring to a boil, stirring once or twice. Add the apricots or prunes and raisins to the casserole, then stir well to combine them. Reduce the heat to low, cover the casserole, and simmer for 20–25 minutes, or until the lamb and rice are tender and the liquid is absorbed.

❹ To serve, sprinkle the chopped mint and watercress over the pilaf and serve hot, straight from the pan.

very easy

serves 4

10 minutes

about 1 hour

Louisiana "Dirty" Rice

INGREDIENTS

1 tbsp oil, for panfrying
6 oz/175 g belly pork,
    diced, or bacon, sliced
    thickly
8 oz/225 g chicken livers,
    trimmed, rinsed,
    dried, and chopped
8 oz/225 g chicken
    gizzards, trimmed,
    rinsed, dried, and
    chopped finely
1 onion, chopped finely
1 celery stalk, chopped
    finely
1 green bell pepper,
    cored, seeded, and
    chopped
3–4 garlic cloves,
    chopped finely
1 tsp ground cumin
1 tsp hot red pepper
    sauce, or to taste
1 cup long-grain
    white rice
2½ cups chicken bouillon
2–3 scallions, sliced
2–3 tbsp chopped fresh
    flatleaf parsley
salt and pepper

❶ Heat the oil in a large heavy-based pan, and panfry the pork or bacon for about 7 minutes, or until it is crisp and golden. Using a slotted spoon, transfer the pork or bacon to a plate. Add the chicken livers and gizzards, and cook, stirring occasionally, for 5 minutes, or until tender and lightly golden. Transfer the chicken to the plate of pork.

❷ Add the onion, celery, and bell pepper to the pan and cook for about 6 minutes, stirring frequently, until the vegetables are tender. Stir in the garlic, cumin, and hot pepper sauce, and cook for another 30 seconds.

❸ Add the rice and cook, stirring, until translucent and well coated with the fat. Add the bouillon and season with salt and pepper.

❹ Return the cooked bacon, chicken livers, and gizzards to the pan, stirring to blend. Cover and simmer gently for 20 minutes, or until the rice is tender and the liquid absorbed.

❺ Fork half the scallions and the parsley into the rice and toss gently together. Transfer to a serving dish and sprinkle with the remaining scallions, then serve immediately.

 very easy

 serves 4

20 minutes

50 minutes

Baked Tomato Rice with Sausages

INGREDIENTS

2 tbsp vegetable oil
1 onion, chopped
    roughly
1 red bell pepper, cored,
    seeded, and chopped
2 garlic cloves, chopped
    finely
½ tsp dried thyme
1½ cups long-grain
    white rice
4 cups light chicken or
    vegetable bouillon
8 oz/225 g canned
    chopped tomatoes
1 bay leaf
2 tbsp shredded fresh
    basil
6 oz/175 g sharp Cheddar
    cheese, grated
2 tbsp chopped fresh
    chives
4 herby pork sausages,
    cooked and cut into
    ½ inch/1 cm pieces
2–3 tbsp freshly grated
    Parmesan cheese

❶ Heat the oil in a large flameproof casserole over medium heat. Add the onion and red bell pepper and cook for about 5 minutes, stirring frequently, until soft and lightly colored. Stir in the garlic and thyme and cook for an additional minute.

❷ Add the rice and cook, stirring frequently, for about 2 minutes, or until the rice is well coated and translucent. Stir in the bouillon, tomatoes, and bay leaf. Boil for 5 minutes, or until the bouillon is almost absorbed.

❸ Stir in the basil, Cheddar cheese, chives, and pork sausages and bake, covered, in a preheated oven at 350°F/180°C for about 25 minutes.

❹ Sprinkle with the Parmesan cheese and return to the oven, uncovered, for 5 minutes, or until the top is golden. Serve hot from the casserole.

 extremely easy

 serves 4

 15 minutes

 55 minutes

Creole Jambalaya

2 tbsp vegetable oil
3 oz/85 g piece quality
   smoked ham, cubed
¾ cup andouille or
   pure smoked pork
   sausage, cubed
2 large onions, chopped
3 celery stalks, chopped
2 green bell peppers,
   seeded and chopped
2 garlic cloves, chopped
8 oz/225 g chicken meat
4 ripe tomatoes
¾ cup strained tomatoes
2 cups fish bouillon
2 cups long-grain
   white rice
4 scallions, cut into
   1 inch/2.5 cm pieces
9 oz/250 g shelled raw
   shrimp, tails on
9 oz/250 g cooked white
   crab meat
12 oysters, shucked,
   with their liquor

SEASONING MIX
2 dried bay leaves
1 tsp salt
1½–2 tsp cayenne pepper
1½ tsp dried oregano
1 tsp white pepper
1 tsp black pepper

easy

serves 4

20 minutes

50 minutes,
plus 3 minutes
to stand

❶ To make the seasoning mix, mix the ingredients in a bowl.

❷ Heat the oil in a flameproof casserole over a medium heat. Add the smoked ham and the sausage, and cook for about 8 minutes, stirring frequently, until golden. Using a slotted spoon, transfer to a large plate.

❸ Add the onions, celery, and bell peppers to the casserole, and cook for about 4 minutes, or until just softened. Stir in the garlic, then remove and set aside.

❹ Add the chicken pieces to the casserole and cook for 3–4 minutes, or until they begin to color. Stir in the seasoning mix well to coat the chicken. Return the ham, sausage, and vegetables to the casserole, and stir to combine. Skin and chop the tomatoes and add them, with the passata, then pour in the bouillon. Bring to a boil.

❺ Stir in the rice and reduce the heat to a simmer. Cook for about 12 minutes. Uncover, stir in the scallions and shrimp, then replace the cover and cook for 4 minutes.

❻ Add the crab meat and oysters with their liquor, and gently stir in. Cook until the rice is just tender and the oysters are beginning to firm. Remove from the heat and let stand, covered, for about 3 minutes before serving.

Spicy Pork with Prunes

INGREDIENTS

3 lb 5 oz/1.5 kg pork
    joint, such as leg or
    shoulder
juice of 2–3 limes
10 garlic cloves, chopped
3–4 tbsp mild chili
    powder, such as ancho
    or New Mexico
4 tbsp vegetable oil
2 onions, chopped
2¼ cups chicken bouillon
25 small tart tomatoes,
    chopped roughly
25 prunes, pitted
1–2 tsp sugar
about a pinch of ground
    cinnamon
about a pinch of ground
    allspice
about a pinch of ground
    cumin
salt
warmed corn tortillas,
    to serve

❶ Combine the pork with the lime juice, garlic, chili powder, 2 tablespoons of oil, and salt. Let marinate in the refrigerator overnight.

❷ Remove the pork from the marinade. Wipe dry with paper towels and reserve the marinade. Heat the remaining oil in a flameproof casserole and brown the pork evenly until it is just golden. Add the onions, the reserved marinade, and the bouillon. Cover the casserole and cook in a preheated oven at 350°F/180°C for about 2–3 hours, or until tender.

❸ Spoon off any fat from the surface of the cooking liquid and add the tomatoes. Continue to cook for about 20 minutes, or until the tomatoes are tender. Mash the tomatoes into a coarse purée. Add the prunes and sugar, then adjust the seasoning, adding cinnamon, allspice, and cumin to taste, plus extra chili powder, if wished.

❹ Increase the oven temperature to 400°F/200°C and return the meat and sauce to the oven for an additional 20–30 minutes, or until the meat has browned on top and the juices have thickened.

❺ Remove the meat from the pan and let it stand for a few minutes. Carefully carve it into thin slices and spoon the sauce over the top. Serve warm, with corn tortillas.

easy

serves 4

15 minutes,
plus 12 hours
to marinate

4 hours

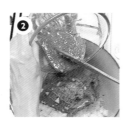

Simmered Stew of Meat, Chicken, Vegetables & Fruit

900 g/2 lb boneless pork, either in one joint or in pieces
2 bay leaves
1 onion, chopped
8 garlic cloves, chopped finely
2 tbsp chopped fresh cilantro
1 carrot, sliced thinly
2 celery stalks, diced
2 chicken bouillon cubes
½ chicken, cut into portions
4–5 ripe tomatoes, diced
½ tsp mild chili powder
grated zest of ¼ orange
¼ tsp ground cumin
juice of 3 oranges
1 zucchini, cut into bite-sized pieces
¼ cabbage, sliced thinly and blanched
1 apple, cut into pieces
about 10 prunes, pitted
¼ tsp ground cinnamon
pinch of dried ginger
2 hard chorizo sausages, about 12 oz/350 g in total, cut into pieces
salt and pepper

❶ Combine the pork, bay leaves, onion, garlic, cilantro, carrot, and celery in a large pan, and fill it with cold water. Bring to a boil, then skim the scum from the surface. Reduce the heat and simmer gently for 1 hour.

❷ Add the bouillon cubes to the pan, along with the chicken, tomatoes, chili powder, orange zest, and cumin. Continue to cook for another 45 minutes, or until the chicken is tender. Spoon off the fat that forms on the surface of the liquid.

❸ Add the orange juice, zucchini, cabbage, apple, prunes, cinnamon, ginger, and chorizo. Continue to simmer for an additional 20 minutes, or until the zucchini is soft and tender and the chorizo cooked through.

❹ Season the stew with salt and pepper to taste. Serve immediately.

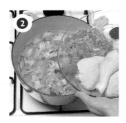

 extremely easy

serves 4

20 minutes

 2 hours, 20 minutes

Potato, Beef & Peanut Pot

1 tbsp vegetable oil
¼ cup butter
1 lb/450 g lean beef
   steak, cut into strips
1 onion, sliced
2 garlic cloves, crushed
2 large waxy potatoes,
   cubed
½ tsp paprika
4 tbsp crunchy peanut
   butter
2½ cups beef bouillon
1 oz/25 g unsalted
   peanuts
2 tsp light soy sauce
1¾ oz/50 g sugar snap
   peas
1 red bell pepper, cut into
   strips
parsley sprigs, to garnish

extremely easy

serves 4

10 minutes

1 hour,
10 minutes

COOK'S TIP
Add a chopped green
chile to the sauce for
extra spice.

❶ Heat the oil and butter in a flameproof casserole dish.

❷ Add the beef strips and cook them gently for 3–4 minutes, stirring and turning the meat until it is sealed on all sides.

❸ Add the onion and garlic and cook for another 2 minutes, stirring constantly.

❹ Add the potato cubes and panfry for 3–4 minutes, or until they begin to brown slightly.

❺ Stir in the paprika and peanut butter, then gradually blend in the beef bouillon. Bring the mixture to a boil, stirring frequently.

❻ Finally, add the peanuts, soy sauce, sugar snap peas, and red bell pepper.

❼ Cover the casserole dish and cook over a low heat for 45 minutes, or until the beef is cooked through. Garnish the dish with parsley sprigs and serve hot, accompanied by plain boiled rice or noodles.

Lamb Hot Pot

INGREDIENTS

1½ lb/675 g best end
   of lamb neck cutlets
2 lamb's kidneys
1½ lb/675 g waxy
   potatoes, scrubbed
   and sliced thinly
1 large onion,
   sliced thinly
2 tbsp chopped
   fresh thyme
⅔ cup lamb bouillon
2 tbsp butter, melted
salt and pepper
fresh thyme sprigs,
   to garnish

extremely easy

serves 4

15 minutes

2 hours

COOK'S TIP
Although this is a
classic recipe, extra
ingredients of your
choice, such as celery
or carrots, can be
added to the dish for
variety and color.

❶ Remove any excess fat from the lamb. Skin and core the kidneys, and cut them into slices.

❷ Arrange a layer of potatoes in the base of a 3½ cup ovenproof dish.

❸ Arrange the lamb neck cutlets on top of the potatoes, and cover them with the sliced kidneys, onion, and chopped fresh thyme.

❹ Pour the lamb bouillon over the meat, and season to taste with salt and pepper.

❺ Layer the remaining potato slices on top, overlapping the slices to cover the meat and sliced onion completely.

❻ Brush the potato slices with the butter, then cover the dish and bake the hot pot in a preheated oven, 350°F/180°C, for 1½ hours.

❼ Remove the lid and cook for another 30 minutes, or until golden brown on top.

❽ Garnish with sprigs of fresh thyme and serve hot.

Country Chicken Braise & Rosemary Dumplings

INGREDIENTS

4 chicken portions
2 tbsp sunflower oil
2 medium leeks
1 cup carrots, chopped
2 cups parsnips,
    chopped
2 small turnips, chopped
2½ cups chicken bouillon
3 tbsp Worcestershire
    sauce
2 sprigs fresh rosemary
salt and pepper

DUMPLINGS
1⅓ cups self-rising flour
100 g/3⅓ oz shredded
    suet
1 tbsp chopped
    rosemary leaves
cold water, to mix

❶ Remove the skin from the chicken if you prefer. Heat the oil in a large, flameproof casserole or a heavy pan. Cook the chicken until golden. Using a slotted spoon, remove the chicken from the pan. Drain off the excess fat.

❷ Trim and slice the leeks. Add the carrots, parsnips, and turnips to the casserole and cook for 5 minutes, until lightly colored. Return the chicken to the pan.

❸ Add the chicken bouillon, Worcestershire sauce, rosemary, and seasoning, then bring to a boil.

❹ Reduce the heat, then cover the casserole, and simmer gently for about 50 minutes, or until the juices run clear when the chicken is pierced with a skewer.

❺ To make the dumplings, combine the flour, suet, and rosemary leaves with salt and pepper in a bowl. Stir in just enough cold water to bind to a firm dough.

❻ Form into 8 small balls and place on top of the chicken and vegetables. Cover and simmer for 10–12 minutes more, or until the dumplings are well risen. Serve the chicken and dumplings with the casserole.

 easy

 serves 4

15 minutes

 1 hour,
20 minutes

Seafood Stew

❶ Let the clams soak in a bowl of lightly salted water for 30 minutes. Rinse them under cold, running water and scrub lightly to remove any sand from the shells. Discard any broken clams or open clams that do not shut when tapped firmly with the back of a knife, since these will be unsafe to eat.

❷ Prepare the fish as necessary, removing any skin and bones, then cut into bite-sized chunks. To prepare the shrimp, break off the heads. Peel off the shells, leaving the tails intact, if wished. Using a small knife, make a slit along the back of each and remove the thin black vein. Set all the seafood aside.

❸ Heat the oil in a large pan. Add the onion and cook for 5 minutes, stirring. Add the garlic and cook for another 2 minutes, or until the onion is soft, but not brown.

❹ Add the tomatoes, bouillon, tomato paste, thyme leaves, saffron threads, and sugar, then bring to a boil, stirring to dissolve the tomato paste. Lower the heat, then cover the pan and simmer for 15 minutes. Adjust the seasoning.

❺ Add the seafood and simmer until the clams open and the fish flakes easily. Discard any clams that do not open. Garnish with parsley and serve at once.

easy

serves 4

25 minutes,
plus 30 minutes
to soak

35 minutes

Mediterranean Monkfish

INGREDIENTS

1 lb 5 oz/600 g vine-
   ripened cherry
   tomatoes, a mixture
   of yellow and red,
   if available
2 monkfish fillets,
   about 12 oz/350 g
   each
8 tbsp pesto sauce
salt and pepper
fresh basil sprigs,
   to garnish

 very easy

 serves 4

 15 minutes

16–18 minutes

❶ Cut the tomatoes in half and scatter them, cut-sides up, on the base of an ovenproof serving dish. Set aside.

❷ Using your fingers, rub off the thin gray membrane that covers the monkfish.

❸ If the skin has not been removed, place the fish skin-side down on the work surface. Loosen enough skin at one end of the fillet so you can grip hold of it. Work from the front of the fillet to the back. Insert the knife, almost flat, and using a gentle sawing action, remove the skin. Rinse the fillets well, and dry with paper towels.

❹ Place the fillets on top of the tomatoes, tucking the thin end under, if necessary (see Cook's Tip), then spread 4 tablespoons of the pesto sauce over each fillet. Season the dish with pepper.

❺ Cover the dish tightly with foil, shiny side down. Place in a preheated oven at 450°F/230°C and roast the fillets for 16–18 minutes, or until the fish is cooked through, the flesh flakes easily, and the tomatoes have begun dissolving into a thick sauce.

❻ Adjust the seasoning, if necessary. Garnish with basil sprigs and serve (with new potatoes, if desired)

COOK'S TIP

Monkfish fillets are often cut from the tail, so the tail end is thinnest and easily overcooked. Fold the thin end under for even cooking.

Moules Marinara

INGREDIENTS

4 lb 8 oz/2 kg live
    mussels
4 tbsp olive oil
4–6 large garlic cloves,
    halved
800 g/28 oz canned
    chopped tomatoes
1¼ cups dry white wine
2 tbsp finely chopped
    fresh flatleaf parsley,
    plus extra for
    garnishing
1 tbsp finely chopped
    fresh oregano
salt and pepper
French bread, to serve

❶ Let the mussels soak in a bowl of lightly salted water for 30 minutes. Rinse them under cold, running water and scrub lightly to remove any sand from the shells. Using a small sharp knife, remove the beards from the shells.

❷ Discard any broken mussels or open mussels that do not shut when tapped firmly with the back of a knife—these will be unsafe to eat. Rinse the mussels again, then set them aside in a colander.

❸ Heat the olive oil in a pan or a stockpot, then add the garlic and cook, stirring, for about 3 minutes to flavor the oil. Using a slotted spoon, remove the garlic from the pan.

❹ Add the tomatoes and their juice, the wine, parsley, and oregano, and bring to a boil, stirring. Lower the heat, then cover the pot and simmer for 5 minutes to let the flavors blend. Add the mussels, then cover the pan and simmer for 5–8 minutes, shaking the pan regularly, until the mussels open. Using a slotted spoon, transfer the mussels to serving bowls, discarding any that are not open.

❻ Season the sauce to taste, then ladle it over the mussels and sprinkle with extra chopped parsley. Serve at once with plenty of crusty French bread.

 easy

 serves 4

15 minutes,
plus 30 minutes
to soak

about 25 minutes

Spicy Coconut Rice with Monkfish & Peas

INGREDIENTS

1 hot red chile, seeded and chopped
1 tsp crushed chili flakes
2 garlic cloves, chopped
2 pinches saffron
3 tbsp roughly chopped mint leaves
4 tbsp olive oil
2 tbsp lemon juice
12 oz/350 g monkfish fillet, cut into bite-sized pieces
1 onion, chopped finely
2 cups long grain rice
14 oz/400 g canned chopped tomatoes
¾ cup coconut milk
4 oz/115 g peas
salt and pepper
2 tbsp chopped cilantro, to garnish

❶ Put the chile and dried chili, garlic, saffron, mint, olive oil, and lemon juice into a food processor or a blender, and blend together until chopped finely, but not smooth.

❷ Put the monkfish into a nonmetal dish and pour the spice paste over it, mixing together well. Set aside for 20 minutes to marinate.

❸ Heat a large pan until very hot. Using a slotted spoon, lift the monkfish from the marinade and add in batches to the hot pan. Cook for 3–4 minutes, or until browned and firm. Remove with a slotted spoon and set aside.

❹ Add the onion and marinade, and cook for 5 minutes, or until the onion is softened. Add the rice and stir until well coated. Add the tomatoes and coconut milk. Bring to a boil, cover, and simmer for 15 minutes. Stir in the peas, season, and arrange the fish on top.

❺ Cover with foil and continue to cook over a very low heat for 5 minutes. Serve garnished with the chopped cilantro.

very easy

serves 4

15 minutes, plus 20 minutes to marinate

35 minutes

Stir-Fried Squid with Hot Black Bean Sauce

1 lb 10 oz/750 g squid,
   cleaned
1 large red bell pepper,
   seeded
1 cup snow peas,
   trimmed
1 head bok choy
3 tbsp black bean sauce
1 tbsp Thai fish sauce
1 tbsp rice wine
1 tbsp dark soy sauce
1 tsp raw sugar
1 tsp cornstarch
1 tbsp water
1 tbsp sunflower oil
1 tsp sesame oil
1 small red bird's eye
   chile, chopped
1 garlic clove, chopped
   finely
1 tsp fresh ginger root,
   grated
2 scallions, chopped

❶ Cut the tentacles from the squid, and discard them. Cut the body cavities into fourths lengthwise. Use the tip of a small sharp knife to score a diamond pattern into the flesh of each squid, without cutting all the way through. Pat dry with paper towels.

❷ Cut the bell pepper into long, thin slices. Cut the snow peas in half diagonally. Shred the bok choy roughly.

❸ Mix together the black bean sauce, fish sauce, rice wine, soy sauce, and sugar. Blend the cornstarch with the water and stir into the other sauce ingredients. Keep to one side.

❹ Heat the oils in a wok. Add the chile, garlic, ginger, and scallions, and stir-fry for about 1 minute. Add the bell pepper and stir-fry for about 2 minutes.

❺ Add the squid and stir-fry over a high heat for another minute. Stir in the snow peas and bok choy, and stir for an additional minute, or until wilted.

❻ Stir in the sauce ingredients and cook, stirring, for about 2 minutes, or until the sauce clears and thickens. Serve the stir-fry immediately, straight from the pan.

easy

serves 4

20 minutes

10 minutes

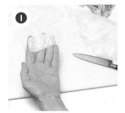

Rice with Seafood

12 mussels in shells,
cleaned
8 cups fish bouillon
2 tbsp vegetable oil
1 garlic clove, crushed
1 tsp fresh ginger root,
grated
1 red bird's eye chile,
chopped
2 scallions, chopped
scant 1¼ cups long-grain
rice
2 small squid, cleaned
and sliced
3½ oz/100 g firm white
fish fillet, such as
halibut or monkfish,
cut into chunks
3½ oz/100 g raw shrimp,
shelled
2 tbsp Thai fish sauce
3 tbsp fresh cilantro,
shredded

❶ Discard any mussels with damaged shells, or open ones that do not close when tapped firmly. Heat 4 tablespoons of the bouillon in a large pan. Add the mussels, then cover the pan and shake it until the mussels open. Remove from the heat and discard any which do not open.

❷ Heat the oil in a large skillet or a wok, and panfry the garlic, ginger, chile, and scallions for 30 seconds. Add the bouillon and bring to a boil.

❸ Stir in the rice, then add the squid, fish fillet, and shrimp. Lower the heat and simmer gently for 15 minutes, or until the rice is cooked. Add the fish sauce and the mussels.

❹ Ladle the rice and mussels into wide bowls and sprinkle with cilantro, then serve immediately, while hot.

 easy

 serves 4

 15 minutes

 20 minutes

Pasta Parcels

INGREDIENTS

1 lb/450 g dried
    fettuccine
⅔ cup pesto sauce
4 tsp extra-virgin olive oil
1 lb 10 oz/750 g large
    raw shrimp, peeled
    and deveined
2 garlic cloves, crushed
½ cup dry white wine
salt and pepper

❶ Cut out 4 x 12 inch/30 cm squares of waxed paper.

❷ Bring a large pan of lightly salted water to a boil. Add the fettuccine and cook for 2–3 minutes, or until just softened. Drain and set aside.

❸ Mix together the fettuccine and half of the pesto sauce. Spread out the paper squares and put 1 teaspoon olive oil in the middle of each. Divide the fettuccine between the squares, then divide the shrimp and place on top of the fettuccine.

❹ Mix together the remaining pesto sauce and the garlic, and spoon it over the shrimp. Season each parcel with salt and black pepper and sprinkle with the white wine.

❺ Dampen the edges of the waxed paper and wrap the parcels loosely, twisting the edges to seal.

❻ Place the parcels on a cookie sheet and bake in a preheated oven at 400°F/200°C for 10–15 minutes. Transfer the parcels to 4 individual serving plates and serve immediately, perhaps with a fresh green salad.

 easy

 serves 4

serves 4

20 minutes

 18 minutes

Spanish Paella

INGREDIENTS

½ cup olive oil
3 lb 5 oz/1.5 kg chicken,
    cut into 8 pieces
12 oz/350 g chorizo
    sausage, cut into
    ½ inch/1 cm pieces
4 oz/115 g cured ham,
    chopped
2 onions, chopped finely
2 red bell peppers, cut
    into 1 inch/2.5 cm
    pieces
4–6 garlic cloves
3¾ cups short-grain
    Spanish rice
2 bay leaves
1 tsp dried thyme
1 tsp saffron threads,
    lightly crushed
1 cup dry white wine
6¼ cups chicken bouillon
4 oz/115 g fresh shelled
    or defrosted frozen
    peas
1 lb/450 g medium
    uncooked shrimp
8 raw jumbo shrimp,
    in shells
16 clams, scrubbed
16 mussels, scrubbed
salt and pepper
4 tbsp chopped fresh
    flatleaf parsley

easy

serves 4

15 minutes

about 1 hour,
plus 5 minutes
to stand

❶ Heat half the oil in a 18 inch/46 cm paella pan or a deep, wide skillet, then add the chicken and panfry gently, turning, until golden brown. Remove from the pan and set aside. Add the chorizo and ham to the pan and cook for about 7 minutes, stirring occasionally, until crisp. Remove and set aside.

❷ Stir the onions into the pan and cook for about 3 minutes, or until soft. Add the bell peppers and garlic and cook until they begin to soften. Remove and set aside. Add the remaining oil to the pan and stir in the rice until well coated. Stir in the bay leaves, thyme, and saffron. Pour in the wine and let it bubble, then pour in the bouillon and stir well, scraping the bottom of the pan. Bring to a boil, stirring often.

❸ Stir the chorizo, ham, and chicken in with the cooked vegetables, and gently bury them in the rice. Reduce the heat and cook for 10 minutes, stirring occasionally.

❹ Add the peas and shrimp, and panfry gently for another 5 minutes. Push the clams and mussels into the rice. Cover, and cook over a very low heat for about 5 minutes, or until the rice is tender and the shellfish open. Discard any unopened clams or mussels. Season to taste.

❺ Remove from the heat, and stand, covered, for about 5 minutes. Sprinkle with parsley and serve.

Vegetarian Light Meals

A light meal is an appealing alternative to sandwiches for lunch, especially if it can be prepared in one pot. Spaghetti al Tonno is quick, satisfying, and made from ingredients most people store in the kitchen. Spicy Meat and Chipotle Hash is a Mexican dish taking less than half an hour to prepare and cook. This section is mainly for vegetarians, however. It offers tasty variations on traditional dishes, such as Spicy Potato and Lemon Casserole, and Fideos Tostados. Both dishes are easy to cook, colorful, and delicious.

Spiced Lentils with Spinach

2 tbsp olive oil
1 large onion, chopped finely
1 large garlic clove, crushed
½ tbsp ground cumin
½ tsp ground ginger
1¼ cups Puy lentils
2½ cups vegetable or chicken bouillon
3½ oz/100 g baby spinach leaves
2 tbsp fresh mint leaves
1 tbsp fresh cilantro
1 tbsp fresh parsley
freshly squeezed lemon juice
salt and pepper
grated lemon rind, to garnish

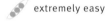 extremely easy

 serves 4

 10 minutes

40 minutes

❶ Heat the olive oil in a large skillet over a medium–high heat. Add the onion and cook for about 6 minutes. Stir in the garlic, cumin, and ginger, and continue cooking, stirring occasionally, until the onion just starts to brown.

❷ Stir in the lentils. Pour in enough bouillon to cover the lentils by 1 inch/2.5 cm, and bring to a boil. Lower the heat and simmer for 20 minutes, or according to the instructions on the packet, until the lentils are tender.

❸ Meanwhile, rinse the spinach leaves in several changes of cold water and shake dry. Finely chop the mint, cilantro, and parsley leaves.

❹ If there isn't any bouillon left in the pan, add a little extra. Add the spinach and stir until it just wilts. Stir in the mint, cilantro, and parsley. Adjust the seasoning, adding lemon juice and salt and pepper. Transfer to a serving bowl and serve, garnished with lemon zest.

COOK'S TIP
Green lentils from Puy in France keep their shape even after long cooking. Orange and brown lentils must not be cooked for too long, since they quickly turn to a mush.

Borlotti Beans in Tomato Sauce

INGREDIENTS

1 lb 5 oz/600 g fresh
 borlotti beans,
 in shells
4 large leaves fresh
 sage, torn
1 tbsp olive oil
 1 large onion, sliced
 finely
1¼ cups good-quality
 bottled tomato sauce
 for pasta
salt and pepper
extra shredded sage
 leaves, to garnish

❶ Shell the borlotti beans. Bring a pan of water to a boil, add the beans and torn sage leaves, and simmer for about 12 minutes, or until tender. Drain and set aside.

❷ Heat the oil in a large skillet over a medium heat. Add the onion and cook, stirring occasionally, for about 5 minutes, or until soft but not brown. Stir the tomato sauce into the pan with the cooked borlotti beans and the torn sage leaves.

❸ Increase the heat and bring to a boil, stirring. Lower the heat, partially cover the pan, and simmer for about 10 minutes, or until the the sauce has reduced slightly.

❹ Adjust the seasoning, then transfer to a serving bowl, and serve hot, garnished with fresh sage leaves.

 extremely easy

 serves 4

 10 minutes

 40 minutes

Fideos Tostados

INGREDIENTS

*12 oz/350 g Spanish
    fideos, or vermicelli
    pasta in coils, broken
    roughly*
*½ cup long-grain
    white rice*
*3 tbsp extra-virgin
    olive oil*
*¾ cup canned chopped
    tomatoes, drained*
*2½ cups chicken bouillon
    or water, plus extra if
    necessary*
1 bay leaf
*1–2 tsp chopped fresh
    oregano or 1 tsp dried
    oregano*
½ tsp dried thyme leaves
salt and pepper
*1–2 tbsp sprigs and
    chopped fresh
    oregano or thyme,
    to garnish*

❶ Put the fideos or vermicelli pasta and rice in a dry, large, heavy-based pan or a flameproof casserole over a medium–high heat and cook for 5–7 minutes, stirring frequently, until light golden. (The pasta will break unevenly, but this does not matter.)

❷ Stir in 2 tablespoons of the olive oil, together with the chopped tomatoes, bouillon, bay leaf, oregano, and thyme, then season with about a teaspoon of salt and pepper to taste.

❸ Bring to a boil, then reduce the heat to medium and simmer for about 8 minutes, stirring frequently, to help unwind and separate the pasta coils.

❹ Reduce the heat to low, cover the pan, and cook for about 10 minutes, or until the rice and pasta are tender and all the liquid is absorbed. If the rice and pasta are too firm, add about ½ cup more bouillon or water, and continue to cook, covered, for 5 minutes. Remove from the heat.

❺ Using a fork, fluff the rice and pasta into a warmed deep serving bowl and drizzle with the remaining oil. Sprinkle with the herbs and serve immediately.

extremely easy

serves 4

5 minutes

40 minutes

Spicy Potato & Rice Pilaf

INGREDIENTS

1 cup basmati rice,
    soaked in cold water
    for 20 minutes
2 tbsp vegetable oil
½–¾ tsp cumin seeds
8 oz/225 g potatoes, cut
    into ½ inch/1 cm
    pieces
8 oz/225 g frozen peas,
    defrosted
1 green chile, seeded and
    sliced thinly (optional)
½ tsp salt
1 tsp garam masala
½ tsp ground turmeric
¼ tsp cayenne pepper
2½ cups water
2 tbsp chopped fresh
    cilantro
1 red onion, chopped
    finely
plain yogurt, to serve

❶ Rinse the soaked rice under cold running water until the water runs clear, then drain and set aside.

❷ Heat the oil in a pan, then add the cumin seeds and stir for about 10 seconds, or until the seeds jump and color.

❸ Add the potatoes, peas, and chile, if using, and stir-fry for 3 minutes, or until the potatoes are just beginning to soften.

❹ Add the rice and cook, stirring frequently, until well coated. Stir in the salt, garam masala, turmeric, and cayenne pepper, then add the water. Bring to a boil, stirring once or twice, then reduce the heat to medium and simmer, covered, until most of the water is absorbed and the surface is filled with little steam-holes. Do not stir.

❺ Reduce the heat to very low and, if possible, rest the pan on a ring to raise it about 1 inch/2.5 cm above the heat. Cover and steam for another 10 minutes. Remove from the heat, uncover, and put a clean dish towel or paper towels over the rice. Replace the cover and let stand for for 5 minutes.

❻ Fork the rice and potato mixture gently into a warmed serving bowl and sprinkle with the cilantro and chopped red onion. Serve hot with yogurt handed round separately.

very easy

serves 4

5 minutes,
plus 20 minutes
to soak

30 minutes, plus
5 minutes to stand

Chinese Fried Rice

INGREDIENTS

2–3 tbsp vegetable oil
2 onions, halved and cut
  lengthwise into thin
  wedges
2 garlic cloves,
  sliced thinly
1 inch/2.5 cm piece fresh
  ginger root, peeled,
  sliced, and cut into
  slivers
7 oz/200 g cooked ham,
  sliced thinly
10 cups cooked, cold,
  long-grain white rice
9 oz/250 g cooked
  shelled shrimp
4 oz/115 g canned water
  chestnuts, sliced
3 eggs
3 tsp sesame oil
4–6 scallions, sliced at
  a diagonal angle into
  2.5 cm/1 inch pieces
2 tbsp dark soy sauce or
  Thai fish sauce
1 tbsp sweet chili sauce
2 tbsp chopped fresh
  cilantro or flatleaf
  parsley
salt and pepper

❶ Heat 2–3 tablespoons of vegetable oil in a wok or a large, deep skillet until very hot. Add the onions and stir-fry for about 2 minutes, or until they begin to soften. Add the garlic and ginger, and stir-fry for another minute. Add the ham strips and stir to combine.

❷ Add the cold cooked rice and stir well to mix with the vegetables and ham. Stir in the shrimp and the water chestnuts. Stir in 2 tablespoons of water, and cover the pan quickly. Continue to cook for 2 minutes, shaking the pan occasionally to prevent the ingredients from sticking, and to let the rice heat through.

❸ Beat the eggs with 1 teaspoon of the sesame oil, and season with salt and pepper. Make a well in the center of the rice mixture, add the eggs, and begin stirring immediately, drawing the rice gradually into the eggs.

❹ Stir in the scallions, soy, and chili sauce, and stir-fry. Stir in a little more water if the rice looks dry or is sticking. Drizzle in the remaining sesame oil, and stir. Season to taste with salt and pepper.

❺ Remove from the heat and wipe the edge of the wok or skillet, and sprinkle the cilantro over the fried rice. Serve immediately, straight from the pan.

extremely easy

serves 4

15 minutes

10 minutes

Spicy Meat & Chipotle Hash

INGREDIENTS

1 tbsp vegetable oil
1 onion, chopped finely
1 lb/450 g leftover meat,
    such as simmered
    pork or beef, cooled
    and cut into thin strips
1 tbsp mild chili powder
2 ripe tomatoes, seeded
    and diced
about 1 cup meat
    bouillon
½–1 canned chipotle
    chili, mashed, plus a
    little of the marinade,
    or a few shakes
    bottled chipotle salsa

TO SERVE
½ cup sour cream
4–6 tbsp chopped fresh
    cilantro
4–6 tbsp chopped
    radishes
3–4 leaves crisp lettuce,
    such as Romaine,
    shredded

❶ Heat the oil in a skillet, add the onion, and cook until softened, stirring occasionally. Add the meat and sauté for about 3 minutes, stirring, until lightly browned.

❷ Add the chili powder, tomatoes, and bouillon, and cook until the tomatoes reduce to a sauce. Mash the meat a little as it cooks.

❸ Add the chipotle chili and continue to cook and mash until the sauce and meat are nearly blended.

❹ Serve the dish with a stack of warmed corn tortillas so that people can fill them with the meaty mixture to make tacos. Also serve sour cream, fresh coriander, radishes, and lettuce for each person to add to the meat.

 extremely easy

 serves 4

 10 minutes

20 minutes

Cashew Nut Paella

2 tbsp olive oil
1 tbsp butter
1 red onion, chopped
⅔ cup arborio rice
1 tsp ground turmeric
1 tsp ground cumin
½ tsp chili powder
3 garlic cloves, crushed
1 green chile, sliced
1 green bell pepper,
    diced
1 red bell pepper, diced
2¾ oz/75 g baby corn,
    halved lengthwise
2 tbsp pitted black olives
1 large tomato, seeded
    and diced
2 cups vegetable
    bouillon
½ cup unsalted cashew
    nuts
¼ cup frozen peas
2 tbsp chopped parsley
pinch of cayenne pepper
salt and pepper
fresh herbs, to garnish

❶ Heat the olive oil and butter in a large skillet or a paella pan until the butter has melted.

❷ Add the chopped onion to the pan and sauté for 2–3 minutes, stirring, until the onion has softened.

❸ Stir in the rice, turmeric, cumin, chili powder, garlic, chile, bell peppers, baby corn, olives, and tomato, and cook over a medium heat for 1–2 minutes, stirring occasionally.

❹ Pour in the bouillon and bring the mixture to a boil. Reduce the heat and cook for 20 minutes, stirring.

❺ Add the cashew nuts and peas to the mixture in the pan and cook for an additional 5 minutes, stirring occasionally. Season to taste and sprinkle with parsley and cayenne pepper. Transfer the paella to warm serving plates and garnish, then serve immediately.

 very easy

 serves 4

 15 minutes

 40 minutes

Chickpea & Vegetable Casserole

INGREDIENTS

1 tbsp olive oil
1 red onion, halved
   and sliced
3 garlic cloves, crushed
8 oz/225 g spinach
1 fennel bulb, cut
   into eight
1 red bell pepper, cubed
1 tbsp all-purpose flour
3¾ cups vegetable
   bouillon
6 tbsp dry white wine
14 oz/400 g canned
   chickpeas, drained
1 bay leaf
1 tsp ground coriander
½ tsp paprika
salt and pepper
fennel fronds, to garnish

❶ Heat the olive oil in a large flameproof casserole dish and sauté the onion and garlic for 1 minute, stirring. Add the spinach and cook for 4 minutes, or until wilted.

❷ Add the fennel and bell pepper and cook for 2 minutes, stirring constantly to coat the ingredients.

❸ Stir in the flour, and cook for 1 minute.

❹ Add the bouillon, wine, chickpeas, bay leaf, coriander, and paprika, cover, and cook for 30 minutes. Season to taste, garnish with fennel fronds, and serve at once.

extremely easy

serves 4

10 minutes

40 minutes

Spicy Potato & Lemon Casserole

INGREDIENTS

⅓ cup olive oil
2 red onions, cut
    into eight
3 garlic cloves, crushed
2 tsp ground cumin
2 tsp ground coriander
pinch of cayenne pepper
1 carrot, sliced thickly
2 small turnips, cut into
    fourths
1 zucchini, sliced
1 lb/450 g potatoes,
    sliced thickly
juice and zest of
    2 large lemons
1¼ cups vegetable
    bouillon
2 tbsp chopped cilantro
salt and pepper

 extremely easy

 serves 4

 15 minutes

about 40 minutes

❶ Heat the olive oil in a flameproof casserole.

❷ Add the red onion and sauté for 3 minutes, stirring.

❸ Add the garlic and cook for 30 seconds. Mix in the spices and cook for 1 minute, stirring.

❹ Add the carrot, turnips, zucchini, and potatoes, and stir to coat in the oil.

❺ Add the lemon juice and zest, the bouillon, and salt and pepper to taste. Cover the pan and cook over a medium heat for 20–30 minutes, stirring occasionally.

❻ Remove the lid, sprinkle in the coriander, and stir well. Serve immediately.

COOK'S TIP

A selection of spices and herbs is important to add variety to your cooking. Increase the range each time you try a new recipe.

Golden Chicken Risotto

INGREDIENTS

2 tbsp sunflower oil
1 tbsp butter or
* margarine*
1 medium leek, sliced
* thinly*
1 large yellow bell
* pepper, diced*
3 skinless, boneless
* chicken breasts, diced*
12 oz/350 g risotto rice
few strands saffron
6¼ cups chicken bouillon
7 oz/200 g canned corn
½ cup toasted unsalted
* peanuts*
½ cup grated Parmesan
* cheese*
salt and pepper

❶ Heat the oil and butter or margarine in a large pan. Panfry the leek and bell pepper for 1 minute, then stir in the chicken and cook, stirring frequently, until golden brown.

❷ Stir in the rice and cook for 2–3 minutes.

❸ Stir in the saffron strands, and season to taste. Add the bouillon, little by little, then cover, and cook over a low heat, stirring occasionally, for about 20 minutes, or until the rice is tender and most of the liquid is absorbed. Do not let the risotto dry out—add more bouillon if necessary.

❹ Stir in the corn, peanuts, and Parmesan cheese, then adjust the seasoning to taste. Serve hot.

 very easy

 serves 4

 10 minutes

 about 40 minutes

Thai Stir-Fried Chicken with Vegetables

INGREDIENTS

3 tbsp sesame oil
12 oz/350 g chicken
    breast, sliced thinly
8 shallots, sliced
2 garlic cloves,
    chopped finely
1 inch/2.5 cm piece fresh
    root ginger, grated
1 green chile,
    chopped finely
1 each red and green bell
    pepper, sliced thinly
3 zucchini, sliced thinly
2 tbsp ground almonds
1 tsp ground cinnamon
1 tbsp oyster sauce
¼ cup creamed coconut,
    grated
salt and pepper

easy

serves 4

20 minutes

10 minutes

❶ Heat the sesame oil in a wok. Add the chicken and season with salt and pepper, then stir-fry for about 4 minutes.

❷ Add the shallots, garlic, ginger, and chile and stir-fry for 2 minutes.

❸ Add the bell peppers and zucchini and cook for about 1 minute.

❹ Finally, add the remaining ingredients and seasoning. Stir-fry for 1 minute and serve.

COOK'S TIP

Creamed coconut is sold in blocks in Asian stores. It is a useful pantry standby because it adds richness and depth of flavor.

Spaghetti al Tonno

INGREDIENTS

7 oz/200 g canned tuna,
    drained
2¼ oz/60 g canned
    anchovies, drained
1 cup olive oil
1 cup chopped roughly
    flatleaf parsley
⅔ cup crème fraîche or
    light cream
1 lb/450 g dried
    spaghetti
2 tbsp butter
salt and pepper
black olives, to garnish
crusty bread, to serve

❶ Remove any bones from the tuna. Put the tuna into a food processor or a blender with the anchovies, 1 cup of the olive oil, and the flatleaf parsley. Process until the sauce is smooth.

❷ Spoon the crème fraîche into the food processor or blender, and process again for a few seconds to blend thoroughly. Season to taste with salt and black pepper.

❸ Bring a large pan of lightly salted water to a boil. Add the spaghetti and the remaining olive oil, and cook until tender, but still firm to the bite.

❹ Drain the spaghetti, then return to the pan and place over a medium heat. Add the butter and toss well to coat. Spoon in the sauce and quickly toss into the spaghetti, using 2 forks.

❺ Remove the pan from the heat and divide the spaghetti between 4 warm individual serving plates. Garnish with the olives and serve immediately with warm, crusty bread.

 very easy

 serves 4

5 minutes

10–12 minutes